I woul  .... this
book to my dear Aunt Bess (Nathan
Levy), who loved me with an
unconditional love, and will live on
through her nieces and nephews.

AND...

- Doris Magison, who planted
  seeds of Christianity in my heart,
- My Penn State University college
  roommates, Diane McClure, Sue
  Zikos, and Maureen Linne, who
  watered those seeds,
- My husband Nevin, the farmer,
  who was accustomed to bringing
  in a harvest, and finished their
  work by leading me to the Lord.

Timely Truths for Toddlers to Tweens

Proverbs 22:6

Train up a child in the way he should go, And when he is old he will not depart from it.

Isaiah 44:3-4

For I will pour water on the thirsty land,and streams on the dry ground;**I will pour out my Spirit on your offspring, and my blessing on your descendants.** They will spring up like grass in a meadow, like poplar trees by flowing streams.

Timely Truths for Toddlers to Tweens

One of my goals as a mom was to train up my children in the way that they should live. A second was to help my children become thirsty for God. I wanted to show them the goodness of God through my actions and through His word.

My first book, **Recapturing the Joy of Motherhood**, dealt with my actions. This book, **Timeless Truths for Toddlers to Tweens**, helps children learn God's word, and see that the Bible is the most extraordinary, exhilarating, life changing, and powerfully truthful book that they will ever read, and that has ever been written.

I remember searching for a devotional to help me instruct my young children. There were many to choose from, but none seemed to fit my busy, hectic lifestyle of raising young children.

Some of the devotionals just took too long for me to gather the necessary materials and to plan the lesson. I barely had the time or energy to prepare meals, do the laundry, and change diapers. How, I wondered, was I going to implement my goal of having daily, life-changing devotions?

I kept looking and found that some devotionals were very easy to use and didn't take too much preparation time. The only problem was that they were written for school-aged children. It was important to me that the devotions were applicable for ALL of my children, regardless of their age. My toddlers were just as interested in learning as my tweens, and so I had to reword many of the lessons in the purchased books so that the youngest could understand it.

One day I decided to come up with my own devotional. My purpose was to use God's word to establish in my young children a foundation upon which they could build a God-centered life.

I began by making a list of truths that I considered to be building blocks. Because I wanted to accentuate the exciting nature of the Bible, I asked a question to introduce the truth. Sometimes I added an object lesson in addition to the day's short discussion. The children enjoyed thinking about the possible answers to the questions, and we had meaningful discussions that often continued later in the day. Even the toddlers listened and especially liked the object lessons that were used. The lessons were quick but powerful.

Ways to use the book:

General Use-
  Ask your children the question about the truth. Wait for possible answers. Read the verse(s) to them, and ask the question again. You may use the answer that I've provided if they aren't sure what to say. Discuss the relevance of the verse(s) to their lives.

-Pick a topic that addresses an issue that you are working on as a family, such as learning not to fear. Read the appropriate verses and discuss them often throughout the day.

-Pick a character quality trait, like learning to be content, and use the appropriate truths, (there is usually more than one truth in this devotional that can be used with character quality traits). Add the use of a concordance to find more verses that fit the trait, and discuss them with the children over an extended number of days.

-Memorize a verse or two each week, and provide stickers, or other incentives for success. (A fun way to memorize a verse for young children is to put each word on a homemade large puzzle piece and help your child identify the words and 'read' them as you put the puzzle pieces in order)

-Develop a plan to use the devotional, so it becomes part of a routine. Suggestions; pick one day each week, like Mondays to go over one of the truths, or gather the children every evening at bedtime for one week each month, or make it a Saturday morning routine to pick out a lesson and study it as a family.

-Read the 52 truths several times within a year to reinforce and renew what was learned.

-Buy inexpensive sketchpads for each child, and have them draw a picture as you read the verse(s). If the child is able, they can write the Bible reference on the drawing. **The drawings in this book are original and were drawn by children age 2-12.**

- Don't have ANY routine. When you have a 'free' minute, grab the book and read the verse(s) and the foundational truth. Sometimes the only time that it worked in our home on a particular day was to teach the children when we were out of the home, traveling in the car.

-Most importantly, DON'T STRESS. Mothering young children is a wonderful season of life that seems to be unending, and then before you realize what happened, all of the grandmas in the grocery stores were right. Your children have grown up. Enjoy and make the most of the moments now, so that you don't have regrets later.

52 Truths

1- We are the hands and feet of Jesus on this earth.

2- God is the master Creator

3- God is our defender and protector.

4- Nothing is impossible with God

5- God is our anchor.

6- God wants us to stay on the narrow road.

7- God can change physical laws.

8- Every thing living and non-living obeys God's commands.

9- Trust and obey.

10- God supplies our needs.

11- Wisdom is a great choice.

12- Rejoice. No matter what.

13- We must guard our hearts.

14- God's grace.

15- God's word

16- God hears us.

17- We are never alone.

18- Hiding God's word in our heart.

19- Do people see Jesus in us?

20- God's love.

21- Joy and strength.

22- Contentment is a choice.

23- God is alive!!

24- Loving what God loves..

1

The Bible says, "We should no longer live for ourselves." How do we do that?

2 Corinthians 5:15
"And he died for all, that those who live should no longer live for themselves but for him who died for them and was raised again."

(This verse is the foundation for every verse in this devotional. We would talk about it often. It took the attention away from OUR wants and desires and helped us focus on Jesus.)

Foundational truth: We are each on this Earth for a specific purpose, with a destiny to fulfill for Jesus, who died for us.

God loves us so much that He wants us to look to Him for guidance and direction each day. I had each child stand on my feet while wrapping their arms my knees or waist, and I walked around the room with them, as if we were one. I explained that was what life was like as a Christian. God wants to walk step by step with us to help us fulfill our destiny. We will become more aware of His presence and guidance as we learn more about Him each day.

2

What do we call God's most colorful design sometimes observed after rain?

Genesis 9:12-17

Answer-A rainbow

Foundational truth: God created the Heavens and the Earth

For devotions I took the children outside when it was dark and we looked at the stars. I asked them who they thought created the universe and all that it contained. It was a wonderful opportunity to explain evolution and creation, and the wonder and magnificence of such a creative God.

3

Does God fight?

Deut. 1:29-31
"Then I said to you, Do not be terrified; do not be afraid of them. The Lord your God, who is going before you, will fight for you, as he did for you in Egypt, before your very eyes, and in the wilderness. There you saw how the Lord your God carried you, as a father carries his son, all the way you went until you reached this place."

Answer-Yes, for us

Foundational truth: God carries us and fights for us during hard times.

For devotions, I gathered my children together and walked into the room carrying a baby doll. I explained that our loving God cares for us all of the time, but during hard times He protects us, just as I was carrying and protecting the baby doll. Although the baby doll doesn't realize it, it is being protected and carried. Although we can't feel His arms around us, we can know and rely on the fact that we are being held.

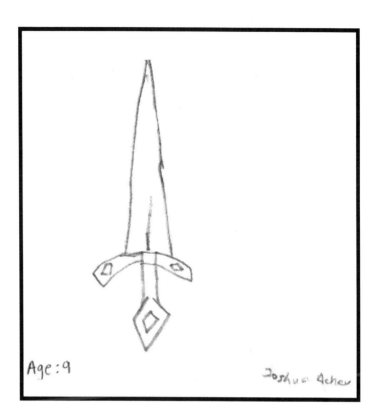

Age:9

Joshua Asher

<u>4</u>

Does God have a short arm?

Numbers 11:23
"The Lord answered Moses, "Is the Lord's arm too short? Now you will see whether or not what I say will come true for you."

Answer-No

Foundational truth: God is able to do everything that the Bible says that He can do. Nothing is impossible for Him

Numbers 11:18-34 is a fascinating story. I walked into the room where my children had gathered, and gently threw a handful of small, plastic, farm animals on the floor in front of them. I explained that I was going to read a remarkable story about God's provision for over ½ million Jewish people. When God let Moses know that He would be providing food for all of those people, he questioned God's ability. The Lord caused a wind to blow quail into the area where the people were camping. The quail hovered in their midst so that they could just reach out and easily gather the birds for food. Because Moses couldn't figure out how God was going to accomplish a feat like that, he doubted that He could. We don't have to understand HOW God is going to fulfill His word and His will, we just choose to believe.

Davison 4

5

We better hold on tightly. But, to whom?

Deut. 10:20-21
"Fear the Lord your God and serve him. Hold fast
to him and take your oaths in his name. He is the
one you praise; he is your God, who performed for
you those great and awesome wonders you saw
with your own eyes."

Answer-God

Foundational truth: God is like a rock and an
anchor. We can hold on tightly to Him. He is
always looking out for our best and will never
leave us or forsake us.

I asked the children to meet me at the wash-line,
and had them form a circle around one of the
metal poles. I happened to know that the metal
pole was secured in the ground in cement. There
was no human who could bend or shake that pole,
but the children didn't know that. I told the
children to try to move it. They pushed and pushed
with all of their might. Nothing budged. I then
explained that God is even more unshakable, and
we can run to Him when we feel unsure, or scared,
or sad, or just need a really good, loving friend. He
is able to support us.

Titus • 6 •

6

Does God care if we go to the left or the right?

Joshua 1:7
"Be strong and very courageous. Be careful to obey all the law my servant Moses gave you; do not turn from it to the right or to the left, that you may be successful wherever you go."

Answer-Yes, He cares. Obey and stay on the narrow road.

Foundational truth: God gave us His word for a purpose, and we should embrace it, be excited to follow it, and stay on the narrow road.

We played a left – right game. I explained what left and right meant, and then asked them to quickly raise or touch their left foot, their right hand, their left ear, etc. I drew a path with chalk on our driveway, and showed them how to walk within the boundaries of what I called 'The Narrow Road', without stepping out of the lines on the left or the right.

Renee Hoy/IN oh age 8

7

Can water stand up straight?

Joshua 3:13
"And as soon as the priests who carry the ark of the Lord—the Lord of all the earth—set foot in the Jordan, its waters flowing downstream will be cut off and stand up in a heap."

Answer-Yes!

Foundational truth: God, the creator of Heaven and Earth, has power over all of nature, even causing water to pile up like a wall.

To explain and demonstrate just how much power God has, I dressed the children in their bathing suits and asked them to pile into the bathtub. We had a contest to see who could be the first one to make the water in the tub stand up like a wall. They quickly observed that it was humanly impossible. With God, all things are possible.

8

Does your waitress look like a bird?

1 Kings 17:4-6
"You will drink from the brook, and I have directed the ravens to supply you with food there. So he did what the Lord had told him. He went to the Kerith Ravine, east of the Jordan, and stayed there. The ravens brought him bread and meat in the morning and bread and meat in the evening, and he drank from the brook."

Answer- No, probably not, but Ravens fed Elijah

Foundational truth: God is God and everything and everyone is subject to Him. The stories in the Bible may seem like a fantasy, but every thing happened just as it is written.

I tied fresh peanut butter and jelly sandwiches to the necks of stuffed animals and 'walked' them into the room where we were ready to eat lunch. We talked about what it would be like to have food delivered to us by a bird. As crazy as they sound, the stories in the Bible are all true!

Hummingbird

Peter age 12

9

Can an invisible army make noise?

2 Kings 7:4-7
 "If we say, 'We'll go into the city'—the famine is there, and we will die. And if we stay here, we will die. So let's go over to the camp of the Arameans and surrender. If they spare us, we live; if they kill us, then we die." At dusk they got up and went to the camp of the Arameans. When they reached the edge of the camp, no one was there, for the Lord had caused the Arameans to hear the sound of chariots and horses and a great army, so that they said to one another, "Look, the king of Israel has hired the Hittite and Egyptian kings to attack us!" So they got up and fled in the dusk and abandoned their tents and their horses and donkeys. They left the camp as it was and ran for their lives."

Answer-Yes, God created the sounds.

Foundational truth: God can fight our battles for us, in ways we could never imagine. Again, as in so many other stories from the Bible, we need to leave the 'How' to Him.

This is another fascinating story to read to children. I had them picture the story using their imagination, and then we used Playmobile men, Lego men, and eventually Barbies, (after my daughters were born), to act out the 'battle' including sound effects.

Elise Hoy i mans

10

What made David's warriors special?

1 Chronicles 12:1-2
"These were the men who came to David at Ziklag, while he was banished from the presence of Saul son of Kish (they were among the warriors who helped him in battle; **2** they were armed with bows and were able to shoot arrows or to sling stones right-handed or left-handed; they were relatives of Saul from the tribe of Benjamin)"

Answer-Some were ambidextrous with a bow and a slingshot

Foundational truth: When God gives us an assignment, He'll provide ample means to accomplish it.

I had my children try to print their name and eat a meal using the hand that they normally wouldn't use. We all laughed as each child struggled with the seemingly simple task. I explained how gifted these warriors were to be ambidextrous with their weapons. God gives us the abilities that we need to accomplish the tasks that He desires for us to tackle.

curtis Groff age 6

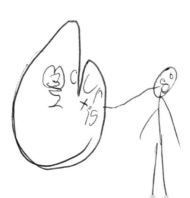

11

If God said you could have one wish, what would He love for you to ask?

2 Chronicles 1:7-12
"That night God appeared to Solomon and said to him, "Ask for whatever you want me to give you."
Solomon answered God; "You have shown great kindness to David my father and have made me king in his place. Now, Lord God, let your promise to my father David be confirmed, for you have made me king over a people who are as numerous as the dust of the earth. Give me wisdom and knowledge, that I may lead this people, for who is able to govern this great people of yours?" God said to Solomon, "Since this is your heart's desire and you have not asked for wealth, possessions or honor, nor for the death of your enemies, and since you have not asked for a long life but for wisdom and knowledge to govern my people over whom I have made you king, therefore wisdom and knowledge will be given you. And I will also give you wealth, possessions and honor, such as no king who was before you ever had and none after you will have."

Answer - He would like us to ask for wisdom

Foundational truth: God's idea of what's important and the world's ideas are usually very different.

I filled a basket with toys, another container with candy, and a third containing a handmade blue ribbon, and asked the children which container they would like to own. None of the children even asked about the blue ribbon. On the back of the ribbon I had printed 'God's Wisdom.' After they chose the other 2 containers, I read the words on the blue ribbon to them, and we discussed why verses 11 and 12 are so important.

12

How should we react when everything seems to be going wrong?

Habakkuk 3:17-18

"Though the fig tree does not budand there are no

grapes on the vines, though the olive crop failsand

the fields produce no food,though there are no

sheep in the penand no cattle in the stalls, yet I will rejoice in the Lord, I will be joyful in God my Savior."

Foundational truth: We should rejoice in the Lord even when everything seems to be going wrong.

Amen.

Titus 6

13

Can your heart think?

Mark 2:8
"Immediately Jesus knew in his spirit that this was what they were thinking in their hearts, and he said to them, Why are you thinking these things?"

Answer-Yes

Foundational truth: Out of the heart the mouth speaks. Our hearts are vitally important to how we think and act.

I showed pictures of a heart and a brain to the children, and asked them to describe them. We discussed colors, shapes, functions, and then what God says about our heart. There are many verses in the Old and New Testaments that explain the importance of our heart. We have to choose what we think, look at and listen to very carefully because we want our hearts to remain healthy, both spiritually, and physically.
We must guard our heart.

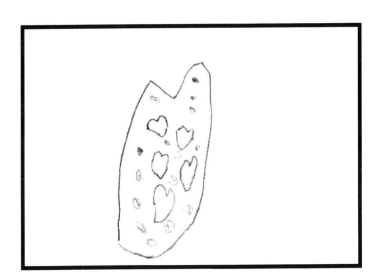

14

What new thing does God give us every morning?

Lamentations 3:22-23
"Because of the Lord's great love we are not consumed, for his compassions never fail. They are new every morning; great is your faithfulness."

Answer-Compassion / Mercy

Foundational truth: God's mercy and compassion are new every morning, or in other words, every time we need mercy, it is there for us!

   I asked the children how they felt when they didn't do their best, or seemingly failed at something. We researched the definition of mercy and discussed how wonderful it is to know that God's mercy is available to us every day of our life.

15

Does God have a good memory?

1 Chronicles 16:15-17
"He remembers his covenant forever, the promise he made, for a thousand generations, the covenant he made with Abraham, the oath he swore to Isaac. He confirmed it to Jacob as a decree, to Israel as an everlasting covenant:"

Answer-Yes

Foundational truth: God's words and promises are always true. He NEVER forgets what He said.

I gathered the children in a circle and said that I was going to ask them some very easy questions, and that I had prizes for the winners. The winners would be the children who had the best memory. I asked them if they remembered what they wanted to eat when they were one year old. I then asked them what question they asked me in the car 10 days ago. After a while they were frustrated. I explained how comforting it is to know that although we often forget things, God NEVER forgets anything!

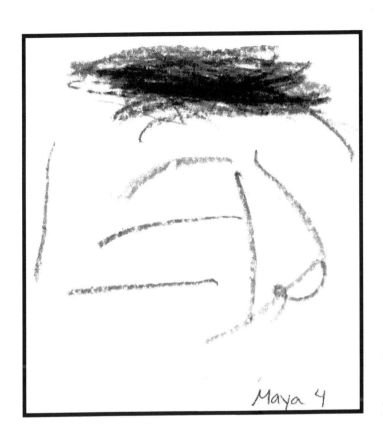

Maya 4

<u>16</u>

Can God hear?

Micah 7:7
"But as for me, I watch in hope for the Lord, I wait for God my Savior;my God will hear me."

Answer-Yes

Foundational truth: God loves me, cares about me, made a plan to save me, and hears me.

I gathered the children in one room and then told them that I was going to go outside and tell them some exciting news. I did, and, of course, they didn't hear one word that I was saying. I was too far away. But, I explained that God ALWAYS hears us, no matter where we are.

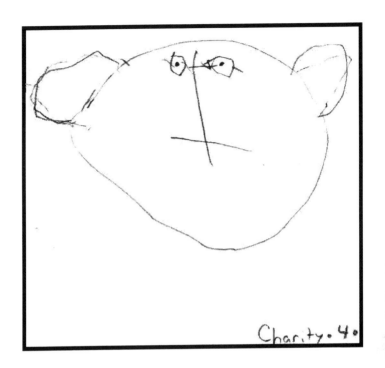

Charity. 4.

17

Are you ever alone?

Zephaniah 3:17
"The Lord your God is with you, the Mighty
Warrior who saves. He will take great delight in

you; in his love he will no longer rebuke you, but
will rejoice over you with singing."

Answer-No

Foundational truth: God loves us very much and is
always with us. We are never alone.

Some of my children had a favorite blanket or
stuffed animal. I read this verse
and compared God's love for them, to their love for
their favorite toy or blanket. I also compared it to
time spent with a grandmother, or best friend. The
feeling that we have holding our favorite animal,
or spending time with a favorite person, is a
feeling that we can have all day long, knowing that
God is always with us. We are each like God's
favorite animal, or best friend.

COLSON

Colson 5

<u>18</u>

Which organ in our body is like a closet, and what should we keep there?

Job 22:21-22
"Submit to God and be at peace with him; in this way prosperity will come to you. Accept instruction from his mouthand lay up his words in your heart."

Answer- Our heart   God's word.

 Foundational truth: We need to memorize God's word, and hide it in our heart.

I collected one or two items that were important to each child, and put it on the table. Depending on their age, the items included a pacifier, a special blanket, a favorite doll, a special toy car, a toothbrush, etc. We would discuss how special these items were and how important it was to know exactly where they were kept, so we could find them quickly and easily. I then explained that 'storing' God's word in our heart was the best way to 'find', or remember God's word when we needed direction in our lives.

Age:
10

Sarah
Landis

19

What 2 words would people use to describe you?
Do you think that you'd like to hear their choices?

John 1:14b
".... the glory of the one and only Son, who came from the Father, full of grace and truth."

Foundational truth: Jesus is described as being full of grace and truth.

How would the people who know you, describe you?
We have a feeling, or an impression, about everyone we meet. They will have a feeling about us. We are here as God's ambassadors to share the Good News. We need to ask God to help us walk in love with everyone we meet.

Titus •6•

20

What can separate us from the love of God?

Romans 8:38-39
"For I am convinced that neither death nor life, neither angels nor demons, neither the present nor the future, nor any powers, neither height nor depth, nor anything else in all creation, will be able to separate us from the love of God that is in Christ Jesus our Lord."

Answer-Nothing

Foundational truth: God loves us all of the time, no matter what.

I asked the children several questions. Will God stop loving me if I am mean to my sister? If I don't read my Bible, does God stop loving me? If Mr. Whoever doesn't ask Jesus into his heart, does that mean that God doesn't love him? Questions like this provide an opportunity for us to explain the message of the cross. It becomes an open door to discuss grace, mercy, sin, redemption, works, religion, and Jesus's death and resurrection.

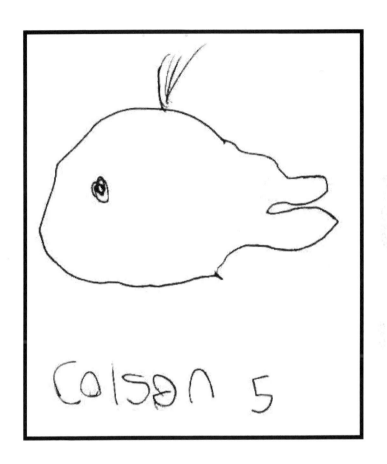

Calsen 5

21

What is our true source of strength?

Nehemiah 8:10
 Nehemiah said, "Go and enjoy choice food and sweet drinks, and send some to those who have nothing prepared. This day is holy to our Lord. Do not grieve, for the joy of the Lord is your strength."

Answer-The joy of the Lord

Foundational truth: The joy of the Lord is our strength.

Strength is rarely used in the same sentence as joy, except in the Bible. I carried barbells into the room where the children were waiting, and I asked who wanted to watch me become big and strong. After flexing, and acting out of breath, I read the verse and discussed real strength and the definition of joy.

22

Is contentment an autonomic response?

Phil. 4:11
"I am not saying this because I am in need, for I have learned to be content whatever the circumstances."

Answer-No, you must learn it

Foundational truth: Feeling content is a choice.

I explained that certain responses and functions are automatic We don't have to think about breathing, or swallowing, or thinking, or blinking, because it is autonomic, (the scientific term for automatic). Our moods, however, are determined by our choices. This verse clearly explains that contentment is a choice. We then engaged in role-play. One of us would act grouchy, or angry, or frustrated, and then choose to act happy. We discussed the fact that emotions are real, and should be discussed with mom or dad, but we can still choose to be content.

23

Is God a statue? Can He move around?

Deut. 33:26

"There is no one like the God of Jeshurun,who

rides across the heavens to help youand on the clouds in his majesty."

Answer-Yes, He moves around. He rides on the clouds and on the heavens.

 Foundational truth: Our God is alive!

I bought an inexpensive statue at a local thrift store, sat the children down, and read this verse. I showed them the statue, re-read the verse, and we talked about the differences between a statue and a real person. We walked outside and set the statue on the ground and told it to move. Of course it didn't. I explained that God is traveling through the heavens, riding on the clouds because He is alive! We don't serve a statue. Our God is the only risen Savior, and He lives today and for evermore.

Hannah 10
Jesus loves me this I know for the bible tells me so Littel ones to him belong they are week but he is strong yes Jesus loves me yes Jesus loves me yes Jesus loves me the bible tells me so!!!!!!!!!

<u>24</u>

Is there a connection between our treasures and our heart?

Luke 12:32-34
"Do not be afraid, little flock, for your Father has been pleased to give you the kingdom. Sell your possessions and give to the poor. Provide purses for yourselves that will not wear out, a treasure in heaven that will never fail, where no thief comes near and no moth destroys. For where your treasure is, there your heart will be also."

Answer-Yes

Foundational truth: What's important to God should be what's important to us!

I brought a few of the decorations that were scattered around our home, and added photographs of my children, and literature from agencies that we support, and placed them all in a pile on the floor. I read these verses and explained how much more important people are, than the pretty things that decorated our home. If we have a heart for people, we will place a greater importance on helping them, then gathering things for momentary pleasure. We discussed ways in which we could help others, in our house, neighborhood, and world.

25

From what does our shield of faith protect us?

Eph. 6:16
"In addition to all this, take up the shield of faith, with which you can extinguish all the flaming arrows of the evil one."

Answer-The flaming arrows of the enemy

Foundational truth: We have protection against our enemy, but we have to 'put it on.'

This chapter explains the Armor of God. I used a cookie sheet for a shield, and pretended that I was protecting myself from flaming arrows. As I darted, I explained what possible arrows could be; fear, temptations, bad thoughts, etc.

Further study- I used other household items to explain the rest of the armor

26

Who is working inside of us to help us to do what we should?

Philippians 2:13
"....for it is God who works in you to will and to act in order to fulfill his good purpose."

Answer-God

Foundational truth: God is working in us to will and act according to His good purpose.

I explained the need to learn to listen to God's still, small voice, and to understand that God is so faithful, loving, and gracious, that He wants to help us want to do what's right, and then help us achieve it!

Our first four sons

27

What does God use to shake the deserts and strip the forests bare?

Psalm 29:8-9
"The voice of the Lord shakes the desert; the Lord shakes the Desert of Kadesh. The voice of the Lord twists the oaks and strips the forests bare. And in his temple all cry, "Glory!"

Answer- His voice

Foundational truth: God has a voice.

I gathered the children and we walked outside to stand within an arm's length from a small tree. I told the children that I 'knew' someone who could use His voice to cause the leaves to fall off a tree. I challenged my children to try to do the same. They yelled and screamed. I then read the verses and we discussed what a powerful and mighty God we serve.

A daughter is born

<u>28</u>

I won God's Powerball and you can too. I'm set for life.

Malachi 3:10
"Bring the whole tithe into the storehouse, that there may be food in my house. Test me in this," says the Lord Almighty, "and see if I will not throw open the floodgates of heaven and pour out so much blessing that there will not be room enough to store it."

Foundational truth: If we faithfully tithe, God will pour out such a large blessing, that we will not have enough room to hold it. Our needs will be met.

I first had to explain to the children that the Powerball is a game that adults play to try to win a lot of money. Many people think that the best way to get money is to gamble. I explained what it meant to tithe. I asked each child to give me his favorite toy. I then ran out of the house with the toys. When I returned empty handed, I explained that I had robbed them, which is what we do when we don't give God our tithes. We talked about the consequences of robbing someone, and the benefits instead of doing things God's way.

Now we are six

29

Why clay?

2 Corinthians 4:7, Romans 9:20-21 and Isaiah 64:8

2 Corinthians 4:7 But we have this treasure in jars of clay to show that this all-surpassing power is from God and not from us.

Answer-Clay is moldable but can be easily broken. The clay itself is not powerful or strong, but God designed us and shows His power through our vessels.

Foundational truth: God is the potter and we are the clay.

I own several clay pots. Some are ornate and expensive, and some are dollar store quality. I read the verses and then talked about the pots that I had arranged on a table. I explained that although the pots don't look alike, they are each made of clay and each hold a plant. Although we look different from each other, we were each created for an important purpose. One of us is not better than another. The Potter decides on the purpose and design, and enables each of us to be used mightily.

My three daughters

<u>30</u>

If we are not thankful for what we have, why do we think that we will be happy if we acquire what we don't have?

Hebrews 12:28-29
 "Therefore, since we are receiving a kingdom that cannot be shaken, let us be thankful, and so worship God acceptably with reverence and awe, for our God is a consuming fire."

Answer-We won't be...or if we are, we won't be for long

Foundational truth: We need to dwell on the relationship that we have with God and with people who love us, and be thankful for them.

We can rejoice in the fact that we will live eternally with our loving Savior! Everything else is on shaky ground, and will never satisfy or replace our heart's desire for Him.

I explained the importance of relationships to the children. It was easy to come up with examples. For example, they agreed that sometimes playing alone with a new, expensive toy can be fun for a while, but playing with a sibling or friend can often be more fun, even with the simplest of toys.

All of us - 2001

31

What should we do if we sin?

1 John 1:9 and Isaiah 43:25

1 John 1:9 "If we confess our sins, he is faithful and just and will forgive us our sins and purify us from all unrighteousness."

Isaiah 43:25 "I, even I, am he who blots outyour transgressions, for my own sake, and remembers your sins no more."

Answer-We should confess our sins and ask God to forgive us.

Foundational truth: When we sin, we need to ask God to forgive us, and He will.

I read the verses to the children and we talked about how marvelous it is that not only does God forgive us when we confess our sins, but He forgets all about them. If we would ask Him about them later, He would ask, "What sins?"

All of us - 2007

32

Bottom line. Who is our real 'boss?'

Colossians 3:23-24 and Ephesians 6:7

Colossians 3:23 "Whatever you do, work at it with all your heart, as working for the Lord, not for human masters, 24 since you know that you will receive an inheritance from the Lord as a reward. It is the Lord Christ you are serving."

Ephesians 6:7 "Serve wholeheartedly, as if you were serving the Lord, not people."

Foundational truth: We should do ALL things with excellence, for it is the Lord Jesus we are serving.

Amen

33

Slow obedience is no obedience.

Hebrews 4: 7-8
"God again set a certain day, calling it "Today."
This he did when a long time later he spoke
through David, as in the passage already quoted:
"Today, if you hear his voice, do not harden your
hearts."
"For if Joshua had given them rest, God would not
have spoken later about another day."

Foundational truth: Instant obedience to parents
is good practice for listening and obeying God.

I read Hebrews 4: 6-8 to give the children a little
background. God desires instant obedience. I fully
believe that there will be times in our lives when
the Holy Spirit warns us, or gives us direction, and
we can respond immediately. We also have the
choice to not respond immediately or even ignore
it. Those two reactions could be very costly! It is
apparent from verse 8 that God would not have
repeated His instructions a second time. I gave
examples, from my life, of times that I didn't listen
to that still small voice, and regretted it later.

Jairus -5.

34

What should we do when life just seems too hard?

Matthew 11:28
"Come to me, all you who are weary and burdened, and I will give you rest."

Answer - We should go to God in prayer

Foundational truth: We should give God our burdens.

For an object lesson I filled up the center of the living room with pillows and soft blankets, and had worship music playing in the background. The children and I reclined on the pillows and talked about how nice it was to feel rested and comfortable. Feeling rested is wonderful, and is available to us every minute of every day when we take our troubles to God.

<u>35</u>

What is perfect love?

1 John 4:16-18
 "And so we know and rely on the love God has for us. God is love. Whoever lives in love lives in God, and God in them. This is how love is made complete among us so that we will have confidence on the Day of Judgment: In this world we are like Jesus. There is no fear in love. But perfect love drives out fear, because fear has to do with punishment. The one who fears is not made perfect in love."

Answer-To live and walk in love, no matter what circumstances in which we find ourselves

Foundational truth: In this world we are to be like God. He is Love. Perfect love is to walk as Jesus did...in love.

For devotions, I gathered the children and did my best to say things that would upset them. I said things like, "I decided to throw out most of your toys", or, "We aren't going to go the park anymore." They were instantly upset, and reacted with anger and fear. Then, I read the verses and explained that part of serving Jesus involved reacting and walking in love, even during hard times. We then role -played the importance of communicating during hard times, while choosing to remain calm and walking in love.

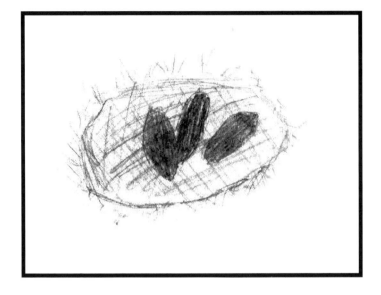

<u>36</u>

How would God like to see us clothed?

Col. 3:12
"Therefore, as God's chosen people, holy and dearly loved, clothe yourselves with compassion, kindness, humility, gentleness and patience"

Answer and Foundational truth: We should be clothed with compassion, kindness, humility, gentleness, patience, and love. They are the qualities that we want the world to see when they look at us.

I wrote the words 'compassion' and 'kindness' and 'humility' and 'gentleness' and 'patience' on slips of paper, and taped them on top of a doll's clothing. I defined each of the terms and gave examples of ways that we could demonstrate each of those qualities.

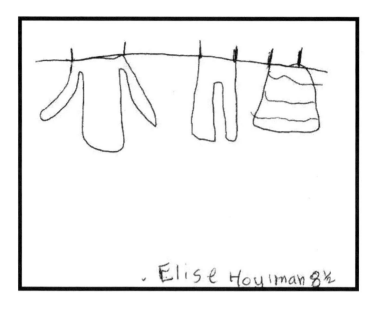

. Elise Houlman 8½

37

Does God care if we complain?

Philippians 2:14 and 1 Corinthians 10:10
Phil. 2:14 "Do everything without complaining or arguing,"
1 Corinthians 10:10 "And do not grumble, as some of them did—and were killed by the destroying angel."

Answer-Yes, He does.

Foundational truth: We are not to grumble, complain, or argue.

God's words are His will for us. If He tells us to do something, we are able to do it. We established the 'Word Police.' When anyone in the family, including mom or dad, grumbled, complained, or argued, the rest of he family could 'arrest' the offending person's words, and gently and lovingly ask them to make sure their conversation agreed with the will of God. (It came down to learning to express thoughts and feelings God's way)

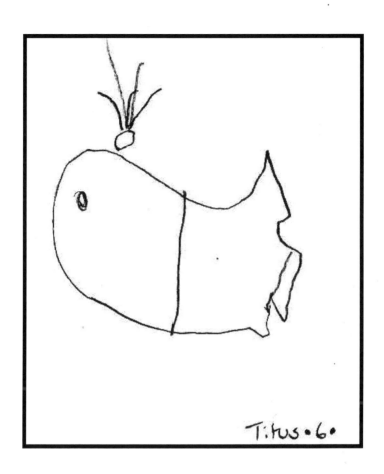

Titus •6•

38

In how many ways was Jesus tempted, and why does it matter?

Hebrews 4:15-16
"For we do not have a high priest who is unable to empathize with our weaknesses, but we have one who has been tempted in every way, just as we are—yet he did not sin. Let us then approach God's throne of grace with confidence, so that we may receive mercy and find grace to help us in our time of need."

 Answer-Jesus was tempted in EVERY way. It matters because He can sympathize with our weaknesses.

Foundational truth; Because Jesus was tempted in every way, we can approach the throne in our times of need, be understood, and receive mercy and grace.

I explained what it means to be tempted, and asked the children if they could remember a time when they might have felt that way. We talked about it, and then identified the comfort of these verses. We can expect to be tempted. Even Jesus was tempted. We can choose not to give in to temptation. Jesus didn't. We can know that Jesus knows EXACTLY what we are going through, and how we feel. We can approach God with

confidence. We will receive mercy when we ask
Him for help.

39

What is the goal of our faith?

1 Peter 1:9 and John 3:16

1 Peter 1:9 "for you are receiving the end result of your faith, the salvation of your souls."

John 3:16 "For God so loved the world that he gave his one and only Son, that whoever believes in him shall not perish but have eternal life."

Answer-The salvation of our souls.

Foundational truth: Jesus died on the cross so that whosoever believes in Him will not perish, but will live eternally with God in heaven.

Amen

40

Does God know our thoughts?

Psalm 139:1-4 and Philippians 4:8

Psalm 139: 1-4 "You have searched me, Lord, and you know me.
 You know when I sit and when I rise; you perceive my thoughts from afar.
You discern my going out and my lying down; you are familiar with all my ways. Before a word is on

my tongueyou, Lord, know it completely."

 Philippians 4:8 "Finally, brothers and sisters, whatever is true, whatever is noble, whatever is right, whatever is pure, whatever is lovely, whatever is admirable—if anything is excellent or praiseworthy—think about such things."

Answer-Yes

Foundational truth: God knows everything about us! He cares about us so much he even knows our thoughts.

Our thoughts are important. The Bible says that out of the heart, (what we are thinking), the mouth speaks. I explained to the children that our thoughts should be true, noble, right, pure, lovely, admirable, excellent, and praiseworthy. We practiced saying things that agreed with this list. (It was harder for the children than I anticipated, so we reviewed the list often!!!)

41

What does God consider good medicine?

Proverbs 17:22

"A cheerful heart is good medicine, but a crushed spirit dries up the bones."

 Answer - A cheerful heart

Foundational truth: A cheerful heart makes you feel better, and is good for your body.

I started the devotions with some questions. What does 'cheerful' mean? What do we look like when we are cheerful? If we are not cheerful, what can we do to change? We talked about choosing to change our attitudes if they weren't cheerful. We can sing hymns, read the Bible, recite verses, or have someone pray for us. Becoming cheerful is a choice.

42

If you knew that God had a plan for you, would you want to hear it?

Jeremiah 29:11
 "For I know the plans I have for you," declares the Lord, "plans to prosper you and not to harm you, plans to give you hope and a future."

Foundational truth: God has a wonderful plan for each of our lives!

I brought out our Candy Land game, and showed the children the colorful, curvy road printed on the game board. I explained that the path on the board is a lot like our lives. We might not be able to see around each curve of the road of our lives, but we know that God has a plan for each of us. That plan includes a future and a hope. We need to trust God for each step.

43

Who must appear before the judgment seat, and for what are we judged?

2 Corinthians 5:10

" For we must all appear before the judgment seat of Christ, so that each of us may receive what is due us for the things done while in the body, whether good or bad."

Answer-All of us, for all that we've done, both good and bad.

Foundational truth: We will ALL be judged for what we have done in the body, good or bad. One night before bedtime, I gathered the children together on one bed, and read this verse to them. We then discussed our activities from that day. We listed them. How did we act? What did we do? What didn't we do? If we were being judged that night for the day's activities, what would God say? I explained that God's love is not based on anything we do or don't do, but our actions, words, and accomplishments are important. We finished the discussion by making some plans for the next day, understanding that we will walk in grace, and ask God to direct our steps.

Elise Hoyman 8½

44

Even the youngest in a home has a ministry. What is it?

 2 Corinthians 5:18-21

"All this is from God, who reconciled us to himself through Christ and gave us the ministry of reconciliation: that God was reconciling the world to himself in Christ, not counting people's sins against them. And he has committed to us the message of reconciliation. We are therefore Christ's ambassadors, as though God were making his appeal through us. We implore you on Christ's behalf: Be reconciled to God. God made him who had no sin to be sin for us, so that in him we might become the righteousness of God."

Answer – The ministry of reconciliation.

 Foundational truth: We are all Christ's ambassadors spreading the news that God is not holding man's sins against them.

I explained that every person in the house, even the baby, is a minister. We have ALL been given the ministry of spreading the word that God placed our sins on Jesus who paid the ultimate price with His life. We then discussed the definition of the word 'reconciliation.' God wants us to understand and to tell other people that God isn't mad at us. There has been a 'bringing together' or a 'resolution' so that we can be in right standing with God.

Gabrielle Zimmerman   Age 11

45

Where can we go for guidance?

Isaiah 58:11 and Luke 1:79

Isaiah 58:11"The Lord will guide you always; he will satisfy your needs in a sun-scorched landand will strengthen your frame.You will be like a well-watered garden,like a spring whose waters never fail."
Luke 1:79
"to shine on those living in darknessand in the shadow of death,to guide our feet into the path of peace."

Answer - God wants to be our guide.

Foundational truth: God, who loves us more than we'll ever understand, desires to guide us in every area of our life, every day of our life.

I covered the eyes of each of my children and led them from room to room. I told them when to turn, when to step up or down, and how to maneuver around objects in their path. I then explained how much I enjoyed guiding them, just as God enjoys guiding us day after day!

Christian Age 5

<u>46</u>

How do we 'let?'

Colossians 3:14-15

"And over all these virtues put on love, which binds them all together in perfect unity. Let the peace of Christ rule in your hearts, since as members of one body you were called to peace. And be thankful."

Answer-We CHOOSE to let it rule in our heart

Foundational truth: God desires us to walk and live in peace, but it's up to us to 'let' peace rule our heart.

I carried several hand puppets into the living room and laid them over a chair, so that the bodies and heads were limp. I asked the children if we were God's puppets. I explained that just as salvation is not forced upon us, we have to choose to 'let' peace rule our hearts. I explained that we are NOT puppets. We have free will. We need to know how God wants us to live, and then choose to obey, even if our feelings aren't quite yet in agreement.

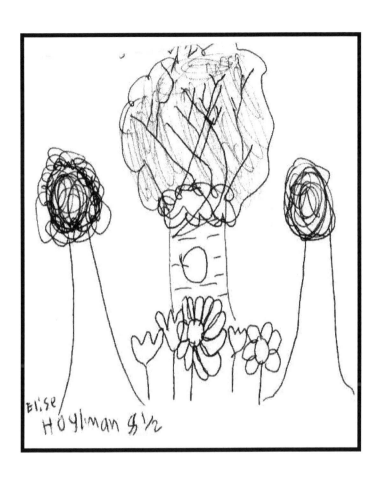

Elise
Hoylman 8½

47

Is a transplant the only way to fix a weak heart?

Psalm 31:24

"Be strong and take heart, all you who hope in the Lord."

Answer-No

Foundational truth: If we can be of good courage, God will strengthen our heart.

What does the Bible mean when it says our heart needs to be strengthened?
I wheeled an adult sized bicycle into the living room and asked each of the boys if they were ready to try to ride it. Because the oldest was only 5 or 6, it was a ridiculous question. I then explained that most things that they would attempt for the first time in life were probably going to take courage. Being courageous takes a strong heart. If we choose to be courageous, God will strengthen our heart.

Hannah 10

48

What is a distraction?

Luke 10:38-42

"As Jesus and his disciples were on their way, he came to a village where a woman named Martha opened her home to him. She had a sister called Mary, who sat at the Lord's feet listening to what he said. But Martha was distracted by all the preparations that had to be made. She came to him and asked, Lord, don't you care that my sister has left me to do the work by myself? Tell her to help me! Martha, Martha, the Lord answered, you are worried and upset about many things, but few things are needed—or indeed only one. Mary has chosen what is better, and it will not be taken away from her."

Answer-A distraction is a something that draws your attention from something else, usually more important.

Foundational truth: We can be easily distracted. We need to be aware that distractions can cause us to be worried and troubled about many things.

For this lesson, I needed the help of my husband. I asked him to hide, but to make noises about every

15 seconds or so, while I was talking to the children about the verses. He turned on the radio, started whistling, opened and closed doors, etc. I kept asking the children if they had heard and understood what I was saying. We then discussed how distractions of any type could keep us from hearing or doing what God wants us to do.

<u>49</u>

What part of our body is compared to the rudder, (steering mechanism), of a ship?

James 3:4-5 and Proverbs 18:20-21
James 3:4-5 "Or take ships as an example. Although they are so large and are driven by strong winds, they are steered by a very small rudder wherever the pilot wants to go. Likewise, the tongue is a small part of the body, but it makes great boasts. Consider what a great forest is set on fire by a small spark."
Proverbs 18:20
"From the fruit of their mouth a person's stomach is filled; with the harvest of their lips they are satisfied. The tongue has the power of life and death, and those who love it will eat its fruit."

Answer-Our tongue

Foundational truth: Our words have power.

I showed the children two pictures. One was a ship and its rudder, and the other was a child sticking out his tongue. We read the verses and talked about the power of words. We made 2 changes in our home. We were not going to allow ANY name-calling, and we practiced saying ONLY those things that would steer our lives in a good direction. For example, we wouldn't say, "I can never do anything right." We would say, "I can do all things through Christ who strengthens me." This is a life long process with life changing results!

<u>50</u>

What should we do when we face trouble?

Psalm 112:7-8 and Isaiah 41:10-11
Psalm 112:7-8
"They will have no fear of bad news; their hearts are steadfast, trusting in the Lord. Their hearts are secure, they will have no fear; in the end they will look in triumph on their foes."
Isaiah 41:10
"So do not fear, for I am with you, do not be dismayed, for I am your God. I will strengthen you and help you; I will uphold you with my righteous right hand. All who rage against you will surely be ashamed and disgraced; those who oppose you will be as nothing and perish."

Answer-We should look to God and trust Him.

Foundational truth: We should not fear evil tidings, but trust God to help with our enemies.

We role - played being in several situations that could cause us to fear, and practiced asking Jesus to help us. We then discussed what it means to trust God.

51

Transformers aren't a new idea! God loves them.

2 Corinthians 3:18
"And we all, who with unveiled faces contemplate the Lord's glory, are being transformed into his image with ever-increasing glory, which comes from the Lord, who is the Spirit."

Foundational truth: We are being transformed into the image of God.

I cut out large pictures of human faces from a magazine. Varied emotions, from joy to anger, were portrayed on the pictures. I asked the children what they thought, when they looked at each picture. We then made faces at each other and guessed what emotions we were acting out. I read the verse and we discussed what it means to be transformed, or changed. When people look at us, they should see the love of Jesus on our faces. We are being transformed.

52

The Bible says that one thing counts. Do you know what it is?

Galatians 5:6
"For in Christ Jesus neither circumcision nor uncircumcision has any value. The only thing that counts is faith expressing itself through love."

Answer-Faith expressing itself through love is what counts.

Foundational truth: Faith expressing itself through love is crucial to the Christian walk.

I showed the children pictures of people from several different continents. I asked them if Jesus loved these people, despite their place of birth or background. They thought so, but weren't sure. We talked about the basis for Jesus's love. It is not based on ANYTHING we have done, or haven't done, or where we were born, or our background. In fact, He does not look at our outer appearance, or background, but at our heart. The only thing that counts is faith expressing itself through love.

You can find Bonni Greiner at:
Mombyexample.com

Made in the USA
Charleston, SC
28 September 2013